History and Invention

The Wheel
and How It
Changed the World

THE
WHEEL
and How It
Changed the World

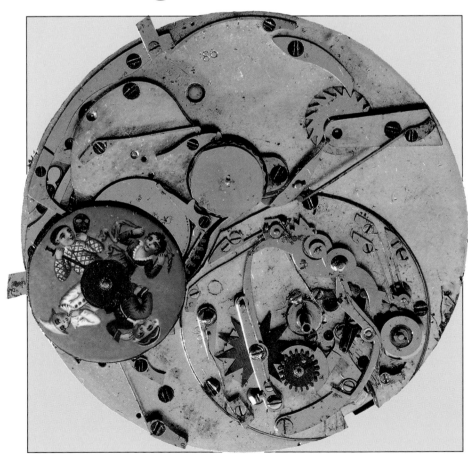

Ian Locke

Facts On File®

AN INFOBASE HOLDINGS COMPANY

Facts On File, Inc.
460 Park Avenue South
New York NY 10016

First published in the United States by Facts On File, Inc in 1995.
First published in the United Kingdom by Simon & Schuster Young Books

Library of Congress Cataloging-in-Publication Data
Locke, Ian.
    The wheel and how it changed the world / Ian Locke.
        p.   cm. — (History and invention)
    Includes bibliographical references and index.
    ISBN 0-8160-3143-6
    1. Wheels—Juvenile literature. 2. Wheels—Social aspects—
Juvenile literature. [1. Wheels. 2. Transportation—History.
3. Inventions.] I. Title. II. Series.
TJ181.5.L63 1995
621.8'11—dc20
                                                    94–15228

A CIP catalogue record for this book is available from the British Library

Facts On File books are available at special discounts when purchased in bulk quantities for businesses, associations, institutions or sales promotions. Please call our Special Sales Department in New York at 212/683-2244 or 800/322-8755.

Printed and bound in Hong Kong

10 9 8 7 6 5 4 3 2 1

Picture Acknowledgments:

The publisher would like to thank the following sources for permission to use copyright material:
The Ancient Art and Architecture Collection: pp copyright page top, 26; Archiv für Kunst und Geschichte: p 22 left; The Bridgemen Art Library: pp 13 left and right, 22 right; Christies Colour Library: pp title page, 24, 4 bottom; Mary Evans Picture Library: pp 20, 25 bottom, 32, 36 top; Robert Harding Picture Library: pp contents right, 17 top, 33 bottom, 35 top and bottom, 37 below; Michael Holford Photography: pp copyright page bottom, 10, 17 bottom, 18 top, 28, 33 top; Holt Studios: p 37 top; Hulton Picture Company: pp 21, 34 top, 38 top, 40 bottom, 43 top both; Robert Hunt Picture Library: p 39 top; The Illustrated London News: p 42 left and right; Image Bank: p 34 bottom; Rex Features: p 38 center; The Royal Armouries, London: p 24; Science Museum, London: p 27 top; Tony Stone Worldwide: pp 40 center, 41 left and right, 43 bottom; The Wiltshire Archaeological and Natural History Society: p 9; Adam Woolfitt: p contents bottom left, 19.

CONTENTS

Two of the major differences between human beings and the rest of the creatures that live on Earth, under the sea or in the air are the ability to use a form of movement outside the body and the skill to use a whole range of tools to assist in a way of living. Humankind is not alone in observing the natural world and carrying out experiments with what it offers. Dolphins, for example, are known for their intelligence and development of skills. Humans are unique, however, in being able to pass on what is known, and use this "experience" to shape the world in which we live. This process of finding out was later called science, and a key discovery which distinguishes the long history of humankind is the wheel.

The first wheel

Many thousands of years ago, humans lived a life in the open as hunter-gatherers, not that different from the few nomadic tribes which still exist today. All the means to sustain life came from their immediate surroundings. In time, it was realized that there was a way of carrying out tasks involving movement which did not require human power alone. It was found that a section of a tree trunk was able to move under the force of gravity because it was round. If the branches and twigs of the trunk were removed, the speed of the rolling log improved. But this movement was possible only on downhill slopes. Upward movement required effort or work. Up until 15,000 years ago with the civilization of ancient Mesopotamia, the source of this effort was manpower.

The earliest movement of heavy loads, such as great blocks of stone, was achieved using musclepower to pull and push, while log rollers were slid under the load at intervals.

As a result of the changes in the seasons, humankind had to quickly accept a mixed diet. This led to the discovery of grasses which could be a source of food – barley, wheat, rice and other plants. The problem with many of these was that the source of food – the seeds or grain – had to be separated from its shell or husk.

At first, a stone was used to split the husks. This process was laborious and uncertain. A better tool was found, the grinding-wheel, which probably originated in New Guinea. The surface of an upper and lower stone was smoothed, reducing the friction between the two and making the effort of turning the upper wheel easier. Holes for pegs were cut into the circular upper wheel and turned at speed. The weight of the upper stone on the lower created pressure, easing the process of crushing the seeds.

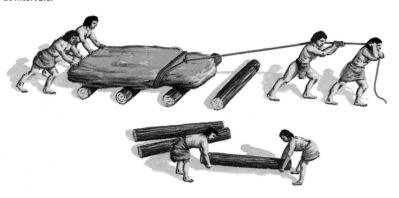

Stone quern. One of Stone Age people's first domestic tools was a rough stone quern, or hand mill, on which corn was ground using another stone.

For hundreds of years farmers depended on simple wooden vehicles drawn by oxen or other animals to help in planting or harvesting their crops. The use of animals enabled people to clear and settle greater areas of land than before.

The use of stone tools for shaping the wheel

Over time, humankind moved on from the use of primitive, chipped stone tools (often made of flint or other hard, sharp rock) to more finely crafted tools, better suited for specific jobs. This change marks the difference between the Old Stone Age and the New Stone Age. The invention of two tools, the axe and the saw, began the use of wood – one of Earth's greatest natural resources. In time, covered, secure settlements were established in many parts of the world. They were based on land or built over lakes, providing protection from the weather and enemy attack. The log roller was replaced by a more recognizable wheel. Bare of branches and bark, a trunk was now cut into segments using axes and saws. These circles were pierced, balanced by a shaft which was either round or square, across which was laid longer planks of wood. This change had two very important results – it made possible the use of animals as a source of power and became crucial for the handling of a new resource called metal.

Pots and potter's wheels

As the population grew and supply of resources became less certain, objects and containers in which to keep food were developed. This was undertaken entirely by hand initially, using local clays or muds. During the Bronze Age, the slow potter's wheel was invented which modeled the clay over the hub of a wheel. In about 3000 B.C., the Egyptian civilization developed the fast wheel, a completely mobile, carefully balanced apparatus of stone. Clay objects were hardened by fire and tools were created to carve exquisite stone pottery.

Iron Age pottery. From very early times, pots, necessary for maintaining life during the seasons, were produced on wheels in forms which remained unchanged for centuries.

Early potter and his assistant. Using a large base wheel balanced on a pivot, which was turned by the assistant, a whole range of pottery was produced.

GROWTH OF SETTLEMENTS

The earliest uses of the wheel were based on the needs of tiny local communities. It was found by trial and error that all the basics for life could be moved with people, and the wheel provided one means of traveling over distances. It was found that if the solid segment of the tree trunk was made thinner, it became faster since the area touching the ground was reduced. Thick slices were replaced by thin. Animals were tied to the early carts and used to move possessions and people from one place to another. By the Bronze Age, about 5,000 years ago, people moved down from early hill settlements toward the valleys as the climate across the world became drier. River valleys provided a water source and timber for building and fuel. Increased population required that more land become inhabited, and so contact and competition between peoples increased. With this competition came a desire to travel faster and to carry more goods for trade.

The construction of the cart

Two lines of vehicles which were to last many thousands of years made faster transport possible. The first was the basic cart whose design was a box on wheels. The box was supported by an axle onto which were fitted the four wheels. This design was secure because it spread the weight of the load to be carried and used poles on which to tie oxen, horses and other animals to provide the pulling power. The second vehicle was the chariot, which was invented in Mesopotamia in about 3500 B.C. and was built for speed. Its wheels needed to be strong but light and to offer the least resistance to air and ground. The framework was made of tough wood and featured wheels with spokes. Instead of being made whole, the wheel was made in sections bent or carved to shape. The rim and spokes were connected together in a central hub, each part pulling the other, adding enormous strength to the wheel. If parts did break, they were easily replaced, and the wheels were soon designed to be fixed to the axle by metal pins, making such changes easy.

The first Iron Age specialist vehicles, chariots used in warfare, had solid wheels, as in this example, used by Sumerian infantry.

Dynastic settlements

The combination of the two types of wheeled vehicle had an early impact on how people lived. The old tracks which linked hill settlements with valleys became permanent roads. The vast forests which covered many lands in which people lived were cleared for fuel, building and objects. Wheeled vehicles allowed people to claim territories as their own, and villages and towns were soon established. As skills were taught, specialist trades in cloth, metals and other materials evolved. Since cart and animal power reduced the number of people needed to grow their own food, clear divisions between agriculture and other types of industry began. In time, protection of property and the community became necessary.

Building of the Great Pyramids, Egypt. How this was done remains a mystery, but it is possible that some form of pulley was used.

The pulley system, requiring only a few workers, made it possible to transport heavy loads from one place to another.

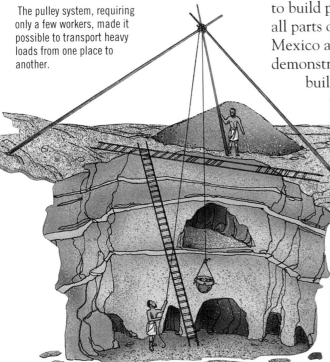

The growth of the city-state

By 5,000 years ago, settlements became cities and then city-states. The urge to build permanent living places of stone, brick and cement occurred in all parts of the ancient world. China, Egypt, Zimbabwe, Greece, Persia, Mexico and Polynesia had great civilizations and superb buildings demonstrating their importance. Almost all the most impressive of the buildings were monuments to deities. Many of these great buildings were built without the direct use of the wheel. It is likely that a broad stone wheel was used for lifting – perhaps as a primitive crane or windlass onto which a rope controlling the lifting was wound. A new use of the wheel appeared in areas around the Mediterranean Sea in about 1000 B.C. The pulley was an aid to building that was fully developed by the Romans.

Application of the pulley

The pulley is a small free-running wheel with a groove on its outer edges fixed by a central, pin axle to an open casing. A threaded rope ran over the groove in the wheel. When swung from support beams, the pulley allows for enormous weights such as blocks of stone to be transferred with little effort from one place to another, by spreading the load in a form of balance.

The applications of the wheel helped to decide how certain civilizations would develop. Much of the change brought by the wheel was positive and improved the lives of more and more people. An increasing quantity of goods flowed out of the new cities, over the new roads and across the seas. By the beginning of the Christian era, what people did and the skills they learned became more defined. This new definition of lifestyle resulted in social structures and established periods for work and leisure. Vehicles themselves became more competitive and were used as a form of popular entertainment. By the late Roman Empire, chariot racing reached a huge audience in places such as the Circus Maximus and the Colosseum. Speeds continually increased as wheels became thinner and the number of horses pulling chariots went from one to whole teams. All over the ancient world chariots were used for racing and hunting.

Development of competitive vehicles

They originated in Kush, Mesopotamia in about 3500 BC. Unmatched for speed and craftsmanship, many chariots became valuable and beautiful objects themselves, as was proved when they were discovered in the tomb of Tutankhamun in Egypt in 1922. It was soon realized that fast vehicles were helpful in war, and all the major wars of conquest from the Assyrians to Alexander the Great involved them in battle. The speed and mobility of these armies over the great plains of Europe and Asia changed the future of the world. Conquest not only opened up new sources of wealth for the victors, but also imposed or exchanged new ideas and skills on the conquered. The Roman Empire, which covered almost all the world known to Europeans for over 1,000 years, to A.D. 476, was based on an understanding of the importance of travel. Control of a huge population and everything from the collection of taxes to law and order, depended on being able to establish reliable communications. Having won control of the seas, they began building a vast network of roads. Many remain as the basis for modern European highways. These roads were 14.85 feet (4.5 m) wide to allow for two heavy carts or two columns of troops to pass each other. They were built on level ground with stones and cement in as straight a line as possible, the shortest distance between two points. The Romans introduced solid crossings at rivers by building stone bridges to carry the roads.

Medieval wars – the use of wheels

With the collapse of the Roman Empire in A.D. 476 the wheel became widely used for war machines across the old empire. For three centuries, maurauding armies battled with one another over religion and resources as the new nations of Europe sought to define their frontiers. The arrival of gunpowder from China and the grinding-wheel from Arabia added to the arsenals of these armies. Coal replaced burned wood (charcoal) as a fuel for the casting of metal. Clumsy, wheeled stone cannon were replaced by big-wheeled, mobile cannon capable of blasting large holes in city or fortress walls. Though known in ancient times, siege machines were improved. They ran on a series of wheels and were made to send everything from rocks to shot and molten lead on to the enemy. Cogged wheels and pulleys able to spread a load and give better control and sighting of weapons were introduced. Grinding-wheels made defensive armor more effective and close combat weapons razor sharp. All these improvements meant that an army could now easily move from place to place. As thick walls were no longer an adequate defense, war in open spaces became more common.

The grinding-wheel, introduced from Arabia to Europe in the Middle Ages, greatly improved the effect of bladed combat weapons. They were driven by muscle-power until the Industrial Revolution.

Diverse applications (artists)

In the late 1400s, some of Europe's best minds were working on new ways of fighting wars. Most were artists and engineers – men like Leonardo da Vinci, Michelangelo Buonarroti and Francesco di Giorgio of Italy. Famous for drawings of mortars, cannon, flying machines and pumps, Leonardo also examined wheeled vehicles. One of the most remarkable of his drawings was that of a bicycle, which did not become practical until almost 400 years after his death.

Meanwhile, di Giorgio came up with the idea of a siege rocket on wheels. Whether this was ever made or used remains a mystery, but it was at least 300 years ahead of its time.

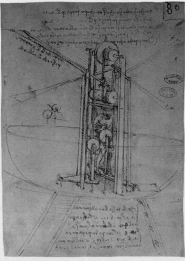

The extraordinary inventive mind of Leonardo da Vinci is demonstrated by these designs of tanks, chariots and flying machines, which appear in his notebooks.

The earliest coiled pots dating from 5000 B.C. were improved by the invention of the potter's wheel. The first craftsmen in this vital industry were the Sumerians, in about 3250 B.C. The potter's wheel of ancient times was large and was made of terra-cotta rather than wood. On the underside of the disc was a socket which was fixed to a low pivot, allowing the wheel to run true without wobbling or vibrating. In ancient Greece, very large wheels were made and the potter had an assistant who turned the wheel until it ran on its own momentum. Up to a dozen workers could be employed in the first pottery studios of ancient Egypt and Greece. A whole range of containers were made, from lidded pots to vases and beakers for drinking. Egyptian craftsmen introduced working in fine stone, and the practice of firing pottery to harden it led to the discovery of the kiln, in which the work was baked. This process allowed color to be added to the container.

The potter's art – basic containers

The basic pottery containers and vessels were based on two geometrical shapes – the sphere and the cone. The people of the Near East discovered in around 3000 B.C. that certain shapes and sizes of container affected how well the contents, usually precious liquids or a variety of foods, were preserved. The Syrians discovered the process of glazing, using liquid natural dyes to color pottery after its first firing (which created the "biscuit") and then reheating it.

Bright colors and patterns of great beauty became widespread, and the vessels became works of art in themselves. Different peoples soon developed characteristic styles such as Greek Attic pottery, Chinese Tang and Ming ware and Italian Majolica. Factory production of fine ceramics stemmed from the Roman invention of the foot-operated wheel and the Chinese introduction of molds in about A.D. 200. By the 18th century, brilliant blue and white china dominated the market, and the great European factories of Sèvres, Wedgwood, Meissen and Dresden were founded, centered around master-potters whose work was copied in great numbers.

The skill of potters reached near perfection in the works of the Chinese, as in the characteristic white and blue Ming vase.

Goods stored in pots

A combination of the grinding-wheel and the press made home rather than communal cooking possible. Domestic pottery containers for ingredients, wine, water and cooking oil became widely used around the Mediterranean from 2000 B.C. onward. This change in lifestyle was one of the most important causes of a division of labor between men and women. Another breakthrough was made by the Near Eastern discovery of the process of dessication or drying, which removed the likelihood of mold, or rotting vegetable or animal matter. The Egyptians brought this process of preservation to near perfection by the technique of mummification, and many of the tombs in the Valley of the Kings contained perfectly preserved containers of foods, liquids and even body parts.

Wheels made it possible for people to construct huge monuments, such as the temple of Bribadisvara, India and Salisbury Cathedral, England.

Building in the East and West

From ancient Egyptian times, buildings of brick or stone became more permanent. New methods of building and decoration were used. The Romans used a number of new tools. One was the simple stone punch, able to give "eyeballs" to statues. Carvings became more lifelike across the world. A whole range of tools were developed, making it possible to carve soft and hard stone at will. Since people's lives remained dominated by fear of the elements and nature itself, the greatest artistic efforts were directed toward buildings with a religious theme. Most of these remarkable buildings still exist, including the great temples of Angkor Wat in Cambodia, the Mayan temples of South America, Hindu temples of India and the cathedrals of Europe. Few of these great monuments of faith would have been possible without the use of the wheel.

Naturalistic Roman statues were carved from solid blocks of stone, using new tools and new techniques. Such skills improved the lifelike effect of statues and decoration for buildings around the world.

The use of the wheel at sea was of equal importance to the use of the wheel on land. Until about the 10th century, travel by sea was based on chance or local knowledge alone. The concept of distance was only gradually learned. Great early explorers, such as the Arabs, began recording information about the sea on maps, making travel by sea easier to imagine. The first trade was localized, with many goods being carried in pottery containers. The use of the windlass and pulley for loading and for adjusting sails of ships became common by the 10th century, but going to sea remained a very uncertain business.

The spice trade

The characteristic design of ships for different trading peoples such as the Arabs, Chinese, Europeans and Indians remained relatively unchanged for centuries. The events which sparked the European age of exploration were a series of disasters, including the Black Death, which caused massive starvation in Europe in the 13th and 14th centuries, making preservation of food a priority. Spices provided one answer, being used to keep meat edible for a longer time. None of the strong-flavored spices existed in Europe and had to be brought from the East. The demand became huge by the 15th century. But even with faster ships, poor steering did not guarantee delivery and inadequate charts made any journey a hazard. Once the Turks cut off the land route by the capture of Constantinople in 1453, Europeans reckoned that sailing east would reopen the market. There was also a curiosity about any lands across the sea which could offer opportunities to expand trade and profit. Ships' pilots had to rely on the stars in the open sea. By night in the northern hemisphere, they could determine their position by identifying the Pole Star which is close to true north. Speed and distance traveled could be measured only by throwing a floating object overboard from the prow and seeing how long it took to travel the known length of the ship.

From the 16th century Europeans crossed the globe in great voyages of discovery. The map marks the routes of the principal explorers.

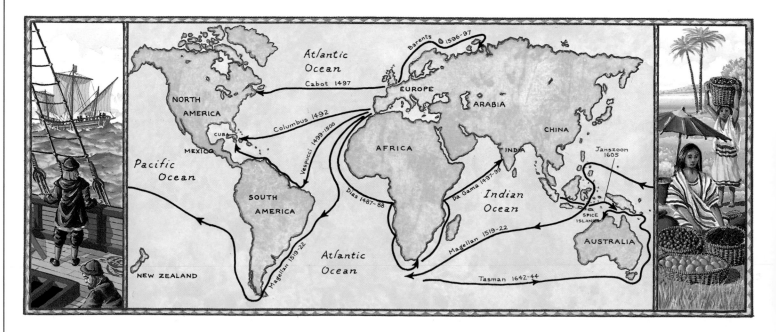

By the 19th century the simple ship's wheel had become a complex instrument for controlling huge ships, such as HMS *Warrior*, the first British ironclad warship.

New navigation devices

The solution to the problem of steering was the ship's wheel. The wheel controlled the rudder, allowing a route to be followed with some accuracy. In the mid-15th century, all that was available to measure time at sea was an hourglass because the sea was an unstable surface. This device was a pinched, glass tube filled with sand, which passed from the upper to lower chamber. In daylight, the shadow of a stick was used to tell the time. When the shadow was at its shortest it was noon. Only these rough and ready methods existed, though they were helped by charts showing latitude and longitude. It was with this primitive technology that the great voyages of discovery began, reaching the southern coast of Africa, North and South America and the Indian, Pacific and Atlantic oceans. However, the achievements of the likes of Vasco da Gama, Ferdinand Magellan, Christopher Columbus and John Cabot (and his son, Sebastian) were greatly assisted by an Arab invention, borrowed from the Chinese and called the disc-based compass.

Early disc compass

The disc-based compass

From the 1100s onward, sailors had used bits of magnetic iron to guide ships near land, relying on the phenomena of Earth's magnetism to direct the metal toward a magnetic pole – north in the northern hemisphere, south in the southern. This principle was developed in Arabia using a magnetized needle floated on water, supported by a splint of wood or a reed. It was found that by inserting a card in a bowl below the floating needle, compass points could be marked out and that this arrangement also compensated for movement at sea.

As people came to rely more on travel and trade it was evident that an accurate measurement of time was needed. The use of candle or water clocks proved inadequate, especially as greater distances separated people. By the 12th century, the science of modern mathematics had been brought to Europe by Arabs who settled in Spain, and their work made wheeled clocks possible. The best known of these early clocks were made in Germany from about 1200. The skeleton clock, as it was known, was made using toothed wheels or cogs in sequence, which drove the hands around. The distance between the teeth decided the speed at which the hands moved, and was first controlled by weights, then by a wound spring.

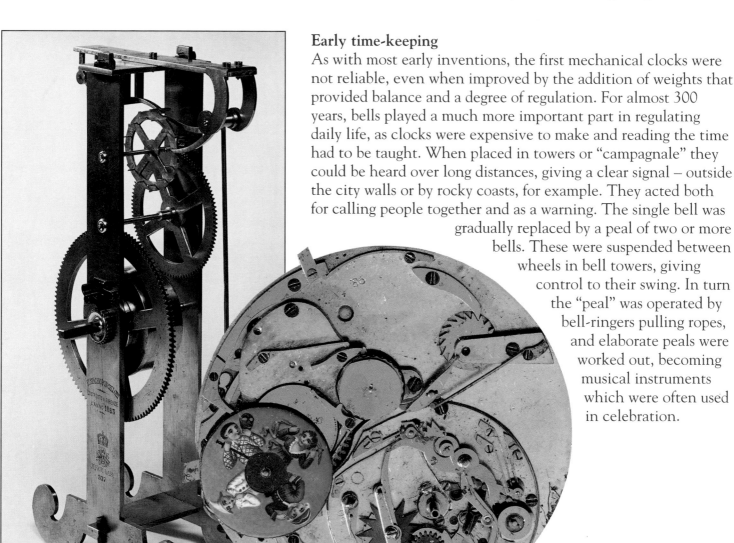

Early time-keeping

As with most early inventions, the first mechanical clocks were not reliable, even when improved by the addition of weights that provided balance and a degree of regulation. For almost 300 years, bells played a much more important part in regulating daily life, as clocks were expensive to make and reading the time had to be taught. When placed in towers or "campagnale" they could be heard over long distances, giving a clear signal – outside the city walls or by rocky coasts, for example. They acted both for calling people together and as a warning. The single bell was gradually replaced by a peal of two or more bells. These were suspended between wheels in bell towers, giving control to their swing. In turn the "peal" was operated by bell-ringers pulling ropes, and elaborate peals were worked out, becoming musical instruments which were often used in celebration.

In this verge-watch from Germany, the arrangement of the wheels, levers and gears of the mechanism is very sophisticated.

The increased accuracy of time measurement
From the appearance of the first wheeled clock in A.D. 1120, the basic skeleton of the clock changed little until about 1500 when Peter Hele of Nuremberg, Germany invented the mainspring, which replaced the weight. This allowed for an alternative source of power, and the clockwork mechanism was later adapted to power many devices, including toys. The erratic unwinding of the spring, disturbing smooth running, was overcome in 1525 by a Central European invention called the fusee, which was a type of conical pulley. Smooth running for larger clocks was made possible by the pendulum, invented by Dutchman Christian Huygens in 1659. At about the same time, cheap and accurate watches first became available when the English clockmaker Thomas Tompion developed the hairspring, which supplied regular driving power. Time became portable and open to the mass market when self-winding watches were introduced in 1851.

Bells, operated by skilled ringers, became a common form of communication until the invention of the accurate clock.

From the 15th century town clocks often became symbols of artistry and civic pride. This magnificent dual clock tower was built in the main square of Berne, Switzerland.

Consequences of accurate time measurement
The invention and development of accurate means to measure or signal time, by clocks, watches or bells, allowed a small number of people to regulate large numbers for the first time. No longer having to rely on nature as a timepiece on land gave both power to rulers and freedom to individuals. At about the time this revolution began to take place, in the middle of the 15th century, European workers were released of their obligations to local leaders, and widespread movement from land to the cities and towns occurred. In various countries across the world the first elements of commercial systems began to take shape. These developments coincided with another revolution which was to change the world and separate the Middle Ages from the modern age.

The new revolution involved rags, water, soot, oil and cast metal. This unlikely group of materials was the basis of printing in the West. The idea of producing copies of images on paper had originated in ancient China, before spreading to Japan and the rest of the East. Carved wood or wax blocks of characters or pictures were coated with ink and pressed onto paper by hand. The work was still done by hand by the time Europeans came to understand the process in the 1300s. A century earlier, the Arabs in Spain had perfected the art of papermaking using the hemp and flax plants which were abundant in Spain. Having built a number of factories for its manufacture, they produced a vast variety of handmade books detailing much Arabic scientific knowledge.

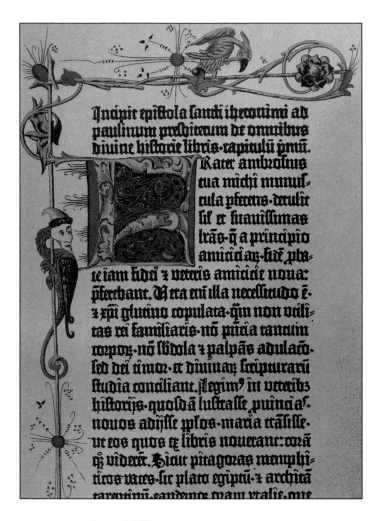

Gutenberg Bible. The famous 42-line Bible, published in Latin, was one of the greatest and earliest of the German printed books and remained close in style to the illuminated manuscript.

Pressing ahead

A German called Johann Gutenberg constructed the first mechanical press in Mainz in 1445. His first books were made by pressing on to paper a reverse-cut, wooden block filled with alphabet characters which were coated with wet ink. This may seem little different from early Chinese work, but, what made the German invention remarkable was that the type was movable. The reason why the Germans succeeded where the Chinese failed was simple. The Chinese language had thousands of characters whereas German has only 26. Any page or sheet could be printed in any quantity using the same letters and adding pictures where needed. The letters were made of wood to start with, but were quickly replaced by cast-metal characters called "type." Few books were made since all the work was done by hand. A wheel was fixed to the press to speed up the process, allowing the bed (or base) of the press, on which the inked type to be printed was placed, to move under the paper. The paper was usually damp to help take the ink, which then picked up the image from the surface of the type. The wheel not only helped in this process, it also gave constant pressure which produced clean results.

The Western advantage

Printing presses changed little for about 100 years, partly because the number of likely customers was small. Even with a small audience, however, printers were seen as a threat to those in power in Europe, especially the

An early printing workshop shows the makeup of the type, inking, a hand turned press and printed pages drying.

church. The church had controlled learning for hundreds of years. The only books were either originals or carefully guarded copies. Reading was limited and the church severely restricted the printing of the Bible for some time. Within two centuries of its invention, the Western press had produced millions of books, newspapers and pamphlets. Authorship became lucrative and brought literature forward as a new art form. With a simple alphabet, the exchange of common knowledge in the West was rapid. This exchange involved little or no travel and was cheap, and so gave great commercial advantage. The value of exchanging ideas is incalculable; print not only changed the balance of authority but also helped to build the foundations of democratic forms of government.

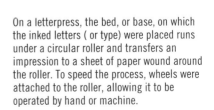

Spread of communication

Just as other inventions based on the wheel added to order and control, printing played its part. The Swedish printed the first widespread paper currency, Germany the first laws, and so on. Mass printing developed by using new power sources such as steam and then electricity, where man controlled the machine. Communication spread worldwide. Up-to-date information was available to all who were able to read and was distributed by fast, wheeled vehicles. By the late 18th and early 19th centuries such exchange of information was a vital support for industry, keeping people aware of events worldwide.

On a letterpress, the bed, or base, on which the inked letters (or type) were placed runs under a circular roller and transfers an impression to a sheet of paper wound around the roller. To speed the process, wheels were attached to the roller, allowing it to be operated by hand or machine.

The use of the wheel as a method of control or punishment of people originated in Asia as the treadwheel. The treadwheel was literally a series of steps or treads built into a two-sided, barred-spoked wheel. This wheel was suspended in a frame above the ground. It was used for both punishment and work, continually rotated by the occupant stepping forward. These wheels were used for a variety of processes, including wine pressing, temperature control and mining. They could also be fitted, by a band of leather or rubber, to a piece of machinery or other mechanism. In hot climates they were frequently used to operate fans, improving the air circulation.

The wheel for punishment

Perhaps the most famous early example of the treadwheel is remembered as a type of firework – the Catherine Wheel. St. Catherine of Alexandria was a Christian martyr, executed by the Romans by being "broken on the wheel." This process broke the limbs of the person who was tied to the wheel, which was stuck on a pole and turned slowly. As the wheel moved the executioner broke the victim's limbs with an iron bar. The final blows, known in France as the *coups de graces*, were sometimes delivered to the chest or stomach, killing the victim. More often than not, however, the unfortunate prisoner was strangled. This punishment was used in Europe until about 200 years ago, especially in Germany and France.

Torture on the wheel was widely used in Europe and the Far East. This Swiss woodcut of the 16th century shows how the victim was bound and hoisted above the ground.

An ideal vision of St. Catherine, painted by the Italian master Raphael.

In the 18th and 19th centuries in Europe and Asia, the treadwheel was used as a punishment for criminals who, under constant supervision, provided power to machines.

Torture on wheels

Torture as a method for controlling people's behavior was in worldwide use in ancient times. Instruments of torture based on the wheel were common by the Middle Ages, including the rack, the most frequently used method for the next five centuries. The prisoner was stretched on the rack in pursuit of a confession, by winding two wheels at the head or foot, to which their limbs were tied. Other methods of torture included the thumbscrew and the wheelbrace, which could crush various parts of the body by the turn of a wheel. Wheels remained associated with death and punishment in France throughout the French Revolution of the 1790s, when the tumbril or open cart conveyed condemned prisoners to the guillotine.

The control of criminals

The control of criminals using wheels took a number of forms. One method involved tying the hands and feet of the victim to the wheels of a cannon and then blasting the person to pieces. Another involved the pulling of the limbs of the victim until they were dislocated or severed, by using two horses and wheeled carts pulling in opposite directions.

Wheels were used to terrorize people during the Middle Ages in Europe. Victims were tied to spoked wheels which were hoisted onto the tops of poles, visible for some distance. The person remained there until admitting crimes or dying. The cruellest user of this punishment was said to be Vlad the Impaler, who ruled Transylvania (now in Romania). His victims were said to be tied to wheels and impaled on spikes, creating a grim avenue lining the route to his castle. He is the inspiration for the Dracula story written by Bram Stoker in the 19th century.

While prospects for trade and wealth drove the Europeans to start exploring outside the known world in the 15th century, the establishment of colonies by Portugal and Spain was equally encouraged by the church, keen to convert the natives to Christianity. The most famous of these conquistadors in the Americas was Hernando Cortés, who led an army from the Spanish territory of Cuba to the mainland of Mexico in 1519. The Spanish had with them two inventions – the wheel and the rifle – which gave them the power to mercilessly destroy the great Aztec empire.

Invention of the wheel-lock rifle

Firearms are weapons that use an explosive charge to fire a bullet or ball and came into use in the 14th century. Such portable arms had come about through improved methods of casting metal and became widely produced and used in European wars. The early weapon was improved with the invention of the matchlock, making it a real handgun. However, it was neither accurate nor entirely safe. It was with this type of gun that the Spaniards began their reign of terror in America. The natives of the Americas – the Indians, Aztecs, Incas and Mayan peoples – were probably alone among the civlizations of the 16th century in not using the wheel. It only appeared on their children's toys. The mobility and firepower of their conquerors rapidly destroyed their culture and robbed them of their wealth. Alongside mobile cannon pulled by horses, the European invaders rapidly added to their arsenal. The wheel-lock rifle was invented in Germany in 1517, the first portable, rapid fire weapon. It was named after the steel wheel which ignited the powder by creating sparks from a small piece of iron when wound by a key and spring. Until the introduction of an improved flintlock in 1635 it remained a weapon in widespread use.

Wheel-lock rifle

Evolution of weaponry

The combination of mobile cannon and portable rifles gave Europeans greater firepower than ever before by the 17th century. By using the new wheel-based power sources, both the number and accuracy of cast cannon were improved during the 18th century. The organization of standing armies and of the substantial national fleets patrolling the seas led to them being equipped with an increasing array of guns for defending the colonies from attack. The resources of Africa, the Americas, India and later Australia were plundered by the armed Europeans using their military superiority. The native peoples were subjected to slavery until its abolition in the 19th century.

Dominance of the new colonies through the use of the wheel

When Columbus landed in Haiti in 1492 he encountered a new people. European meetings with other peoples such as the Chinese or Indians had generally resulted in a mutual understanding, once purely religious differences were put aside. In the Americas, the Spanish and Portuguese (and later the English and French) brought with them not only their advanced technology, but also a deadly combination of greed, religious zeal and disease. Having attacked and overpowered the natives, the Spanish and Portuguese set about enslaving them, forcing them to work in local silver mines using all the advantages of the wheel, as used in production at home. Spain had mortgaged much of this wealth within a century, to defend her possessions against competitors. In the process the great civilizations of South America had been destroyed, the cities levelled and minerals plundered.

Trade in slaves from Africa began after da Gama's exporation of the African coasts in the late 15th century. These slaves endured some of the most inhumane conditions ever imposed by one race on another. This terrible trade was to last almost four hundred years and in time be one of the factors setting off the American Civil War in the 1860s. Many of the later colonies of Europeans took with them their wheeled technology and its products, relying on the vast lands they claimed to provide them with raw materials. Mostly gathered by slave labor, raw materials such as cotton or sugar became the staples for the new Western industries, further adding to their wealth and power. In turn, the status of the native peoples declined. Mass production of wheeled vehicles and the introduction of railways led to the means to destroy or transport the products of their native environment and condemned them to an unequal relationship with Europeans. There were a number who failed to survive the onslaught at all – the aborigines of Tasmania and Tierra del Fuego being two examples among many.

Slavery was widespread in the tropics for hundreds of years. Blacks were seized by traders who sold their unfortunate captives to Europeans, to be transported to the Colonies.

Ancient Arab inventions based on the wheel made survival possible in lands where water was scarce. It had long been known that water existed deep underground and could be reached by drilling holes, and creating artificial lakes, or taken from rivers and sprinkled over dry land. Once a water source was found, the Arabs built a huge wheel with a number of buckets fitted around the rim, which was partly submerged.

The wheel was connected with an axle and then to a type of capstan (a thick revolving cylinder) which was turned by a camel, raising bucket after bucket. Arabs also used a waterwheel in slow-running rivers, placed below waterfalls for irrigation. These simple devices were adapted in the West, to make use of the abundant water in northern Europe. The watermill became a major component of the Industrial Revolution of the 18th century, which began in Britain.

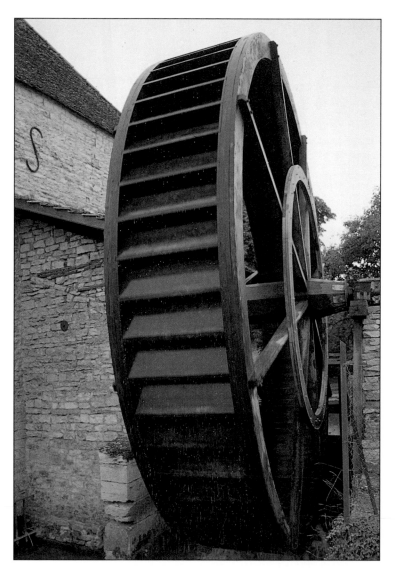

Broad waterwheels became a common sight along streams and rivers in Europe, and became a key element in the development of the Industrial Revolution.

The early waterwheel

The European waterwheel was devised not for irrigation or water supply, but to provide a source of power for the production of cloth. Since water was used in a number of the processes leading from raw cotton to cloth, the industries were sited on rivers or fast-flowing streams. The power of the water hit the broad blades of the wheel with full force, driving it around. In about 1750, an Englishman called James Brindley began to improve the working of the wheels and cogs which drove the internal machinery of the mill and so increased production. By chance, it was found that Britain had another valuable energy resource – coal.

Applications of the waterwheel

With new methods of smelting iron using coal, by separating the metal from impurities to produce a tough, versatile material, it was possible to mass produce everyday objects for the home and overseas markets. However, it was necessary to improve safety in the mines, especially to reduce the danger of flooding, to ensure a constant supply of coal. Wheels had been used in mines for centuries, providing the wheels of trucks which transported the coal or ore, and for operating the winding gear which lowered animals, men and their equipment into the pits or brought them back out again. Old hand-pumps now proved unreliable as they lacked the power needed to shift large volumes of floodwater. The solution was provided by John Newcomen, who developed a pumping engine powered by steam which used a rotating wheel as the basis for operating the pump.

Newcomen's Engine. A Newcomen steam engine used a wheel and chain drive to control the giant beam and careful timing mechanism. Until Watt's improvements, it was the best engine available to drain flooded mines.

The windmill evolved in different ways in different countries. Crucial for pumping, irrigation, drainage and the grinding of corn, it was adapted to different climates and technology. The traditional Dutch mill, the Mediterranean mill, the Prairie mill of North America and the modern power mill, which generates electricity, were designed to meet varying local conditions.

How the power wheel affected everyday life

The combination of the pumping-engine and the waterwheel helped establish or improve four major industries in Britain – mining, clothing, food and smelting. Neither invention provided ideal solutions to meet the demand for constant power in the long run – the pumping-engine had variable motion and the waterwheels were useless when the river ran dry. However, employment was encouraged through their use. That fewer people were required on the land was evident. Even where continued employment was uncertain, the new factory system established organized labor on a scale far greater than had been seen before. The new industries also created competition for money and assets. This led to the widespread availability of a national currency, to be spent as people wished on an ever increasing range of goods. By 1770, everyday items such as clothing, glass, cutlery and china were available at low cost to the majority of Britain's population, together with a surplus of goods for export.

With the discovery by Europeans of the new lands across the oceans in the East and West, mariners needed to be able to pinpoint their position at sea. The solution to the problem came from an English genius called Isaac Newton. He had discovered the simple principle that since the sun goes around the Earth in 24 hours, each of the 360 degrees of longitude occupies four minutes of time. Therefore, if a sailor could keep accurate time on board ship and compare it with the time at a point on the earth with a defined longitude, he would know precisely the distance over which he had traveled. Having established an observatory at Greenwich, the British designated the line of longitude which ran through this outpost of London as "Greenwich Mean Time." This line became the reference point from which time at sea would be measured.

The invention of the chronometer

In 1713, the British government offered a prize of £20,000 (in 1994: $30,000) for a timekeeper which would prove accurate to half a degree on a voyage of six weeks. The eventual winner was John Harrison who invented a chronometer (or navigational clock) and sent his son to Jamaica to test the device. It lost only 114.5 seconds on the voyage, well within the margin of error. This new clock was remarkable in several ways. It used a device to alter the compensation in the running of the clock's wheels according to the temperature, and also included several pendulums (rods with weights) which regulated the clockwork motion of the chronometer, which corrected for the lurch of the ship. The use of such instruments gave traders their first accurate readings for the position of their vessels, and the relative position of one vessel to another. Not only did this help to establish specific trade routes and allow for increased accuracy of maps and charts, it also introduced the idea of relative time, a notion which had a profound effect on the world two centuries later.

Harrison's chronometer

The wheel in control of the elements

By the 12th century, the windmill had arrived in Europe from Asia. This used sails powered by the wind and connected by a main axle and geared wheels to water-pumps. The problem of seasonal flooding of lowlands could now be controlled. Canals for irrigation and drainage were dug at about the same time. The potential of these waterways for use in trade by small ships and barges remained limited until the 1760s. The eccentric Duke of Bridgewater then asked an engineer called James Brindley to build a canal to carry coal from his English estate to Manchester. The scheme worked. Within twelve years, 260 miles of English canals linked a range of natural resources to the markets. Due to the terrain in many places, water had to go uphill as well as down. Brindley's solution was to build stepped compartments, or locks, sealed by gates. Both the gates and the flow of water through the sluices were controlled by wheels which could be turned easily by one man. It proved to be a brilliant answer.

Accurate navigation increased the range and speed of ships. By the 20th century, sailing ships, such as the clipper, were trading goods across the world's oceans in a shorter and shorter time.

Britain developed a network of canals as water highways across the country in the 18th and 19th centuries, linking many products to the markets of the leading towns and cities.

The subsequent expansion of trade

As with many new schemes, the idea that canals could change a country and then affect how the whole world lived would have been fantastic in the 18th century. Yet, from the wishes of a strange duke, England developed a tried and tested system for the rapid movement of the resources on which the Industrial Revolution depended. Not only was it simple to have water highways, it was also cheap and entirely flexible. Raw materials and goods could now be directly transported in large quantities from the factory right into the center of cities. The supremacy of canals was to last only 60 years in Britain and a little longer on the continent. Their use was challenged by a new and awesome machine called the steam engine.

The idea of using steam as a power source had interested man for centuries. In the 1600s for example, both the English and French made simple steam-driven machines. Newcomen's steam-pumping engines, which used the principle of a beam drive and a wheel control for pressure, caught the attention of young Scotsman James Watt in 1768. He began to build his own steam engine for pumping water. His initial experiment failed and as a result his rights in the work were considered worthless and passed to a Birmingham metal worker called Matthew Boulton. After ten years work, paid for by Boulton, Watt devised a new principle for the steam engine in 1781. Watt devised a rotary system to replace the beam drive. The invention marked the beginning of the steam age.

STEAM POWER

The Watt-Boulton engine was based on a very simple device, called the sun and planet gear. The small, geared wheel (the planet) revolved around another geared wheel (the sun) which was itself on the same axle as the larger driving wheel. Steam was driven into the piston chamber, expanded and turned the wheel, and as the wheel dropped, the piston expelled the steam from the chamber. The wheel in turn drove the machinery being used. Due to the limited advances in the making of metals, all Watt's engines were low-pressure, and while the machines produced immense power (which Watt himself named horse power) they were used for large-scale operations only.

Stevenson's first locomotive of 1825 demonstrated that iron wheels with pistons were a practical and effective form of transport.

S.&.D.R. N°I. 1825.

The spinning jenny

World population had grown rapidly by 1720 and demand for clothing rocketed. Across the world, however, the basic technology of the spinning wheel had remained virtually unchanged since its invention in India in about 1000 B.C. Small cottage industries were unable to meet demand, especially in Europe. The solution was automation. A whole series of wheel-based inventions, ranging from Arkwright's spinning machine to Hargreave's spinning jenny, rapidly increased production. The old industry was wiped out within thirty years, and the new factories sprang up all across the developed world, enslaving many people in long days of ceaseless and sometimes dangerous work. A new way of life called capitalism was born.

The spinning jenny was one of the series of machines which revolutionized the manufacture of cloth from the 18th century, creating a new industry.

The first railways

The principle of the straight track which gave least resistance to the wheel was well established by the 19th century. In 1802, a Cornishman called Richard Trevithick devised an engine powered by steam to run along a railway line, pulling goods in trucks at an iron works in Wales. Since the iron track split, the experiment was abandoned and more or less forgotten. The next development, the rack, cogged railway, was overtaken by the work of George Stevenson and his son Robert in England.

The world's first public railway to use the piston and steam engine to drive the wheels, ran from Stockton to Darlington in 1826. Stevenson found that the pitch of the engine was minimized by using six wheels, which became a standard design. Railways spread rapidly through the world as the most reliable and effective means of land transport. They played a huge part in making long journeys easier in countries such as Canada, in peace and in war. The Crimean War of the 1850s and the American Civil War of the 1860s are good examples of where railways played a decisive part in the victory.

A steam engine relies on a constant supply of steam, produced as a result of burning coal to heat water. In a locomotive, the steam, under great pressure, is forced through to pistons which drive the banks of wheels.

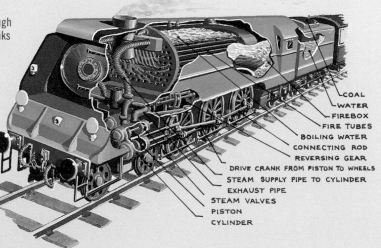

COAL
WATER
FIREBOX
FIRE TUBES
BOILING WATER
CONNECTING ROD
REVERSING GEAR
DRIVE CRANK FROM PISTON TO WHEELS
STEAM SUPPLY PIPE TO CYLINDER
EXHAUST PIPE
STEAM VALVES
PISTON
CYLINDER

The world changed as a result of the Industrial Revolution in England due to a number of ideas, discoveries and inventions coming together at roughly the same time. Though connected with work, production and a way of life, for good or bad all these events had a common theme – control. As people investigated the natural world about them, their association with it altered. Knowledge and information helped to set aside the old fears. Early in the 19th century, people in the West believed they could control their destiny if they could control the forces of nature. Much early machinery was based on the human invention of the wheel, and demonstrated that such power might be possible.

Sizable flywheel

James Watt had realized that when a wheel covers a certain distance and time it also stores up energy in the process. For his first steam engines, Watt devised a flywheel (a heavy wheel on a revolving shaft) to make the machines keep a regular speed. The invention proved the perfect solution for a whole range of machines which needed to work at constant, known speeds. Watt did not claim ownership or patent this idea. This was a personal mistake, but was of great benefit to the world as a whole. The energy or power of any given machine was now controllable. At the beginning of the 19th century, it was soon found that the flywheel had to be made with curved spokes to absorb pressure, otherwise it was known to "run away," destroying not only the machine, but also the lives of those working near it. A hand-operated wheel easily shows that it stores energy, continuing regular movement. After a certain number of turns it can be let go and will continue to turn, using the stored energy within it.

The use of flywheels in clocks and watches

The flywheel in clocks and watches performs a similar function to that of the wheel in other machines. It is sometimes known as the "compensating balance" and is an ingenious controlling device. It regulates not only the movement of the watch or clock by maintaining a constant speed, but also the temperature. The flywheel has two sets of spokes joined back to back (one pointing inward and the

other outward), which are made of two different metals, steel and brass. In cold temperatures the spokes shorten, in hot they expand. This keeps the leverage of the rim relative to the drive wheel constant.

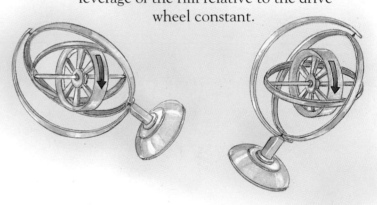

The discovery of the flywheel made accurate regulation of clocks possible. The later invention of the conical fusee control in Czechoslovakia improved such regulation.

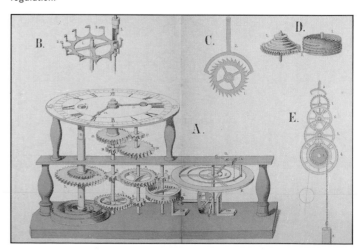

The *Great Eastern*, designed by master engineer Isambard Kingdom Brunel and financed by a railway company, used both sail and steampower, transporting both emigrants and goods across the Atlantic in the 19th century. Powered by a pair of huge paddle wheels, it achieved record speeds for the crossing.

Benefits for the world

The benefits of the flywheel were immediate. The new accuracy in measuring time, and improved safety of the machines, allowed for an ordered way of life and for work and leisure to be adopted. Publications now included times for the start and finish of events. People were able to organize their lives with more certainty. Cities expanded around centers of communication, such as ports and railways, so the idea of timetables for travel allowed people to choose their destination. At the same time, the flywheel increased confidence and security in industry by making machines safer, extending to the defense of the nation and its interests.

New applications and services

Within a hundred years of the first use of the flywheel, it appeared in a whole range of engines covering every aspect of life. Such machines included water turbines, presses, shearers, punching and slotting machines, forges, crushers, rolling mills, electric generators, the internal combustion engine, clocks, watches, timekeepers, steamships and railways. Wherever anything needed to be changed, moved or begun by powered mechanical means there was a flywheel in some shape or form. Many items which had been luxuries became common and added to the quality of life in industrial nations. These included running water, electric lighting, fresh food from all over the world, mass circulation newspapers and a daily postal service. Such new services created huge advantages for the industrial nations, especially Britain. By backing its inventors, creating organizations such as the civil service to administer its commerce and by maintaining a powerful navy to keep trade routes open, Britain controlled two-thirds of the world's surface in a huge empire by the end of the 19th century.

The modern electronics-based newspaper office grew out of the applications of the flywheel which made modern commercial life possible and encouraged the development of new products and services throughout the world.

The flywheel served as a means of protection to both man and machine. The wheel was also used to increase safety in other ways. From the earliest civilizations onward, there had been an interest in the natural chemicals which made up the world. Those which were of use and those which were harmful were gradually identified. In the Middle Ages, the search for new wealth spurred a renewed investigation of the chemical elements and a number were identified. These investigators were first called "alchemists" but were soon known as "natural philosophers" and became known as chemists by the late 18th century.

From the first use of anesthetics in surgery, such as this operation performed by Lister, containers for the safekeeping of dangerous gases and liquids were introduced, eventually becoming a vital element of modern medicine.

The wheel as protection

Extracts from plants and animals had long been used for medicine, but it was chemists who unraveled the mysteries of the elements and compounds of which these substances are made. Some of the new discoveries, such as soda ash or gases, were to have very important applications. Yet even in the middle of the 19th century, it was not fully realized that some of these materials needed special containers. The first gas plants were founded around 1800, used for lighting and heating. But bottled gas remained unavailable for 50 years. When steel cylinders with a wheel controlling the valve at the head of the container were invented in America in the 1860s, it was then realized that many possibilities were opened up. The discovery of commercial quantities of oil by Colonel Edwin Drake in America in 1859 speeded up the use of wheel-topped cylinders and wheel-based pipes. "Laughing gas" was used as an anesthetic in an operation for the first time in 1846, protecting a patient during surgery. The gas was contained in the wheel-controlled bottles.

By the 1960s huge vaults had been built for banks, locking away valuables behind virtually impenetrable steel doors, often controlled by wheels.

The wheeled hatch of the submarine, often placed in the conning tower, made underwater living possible.

The wheel as lock or control
The sea was not examined in detail until the 19th century, when scientists, such as Thomas Huxley, and Western navies became interested in its exploration. By 1860, submarine craft had been tested for almost 200 years. The British and American navies built the first modern submarines during the American Civil War. A watertight vessel needed to be built with openings which could be sealed fast. The solution was a lock controlled by a wheel. It proved to work almost perfectly under pressurized conditions and remains in use on submarines to the present day. The same principle was applied to deep-sea diving, allowing a controlled flow of air to reach a diver from a surface ship. The idea of wheel-based locks or controls spread to a whole range of equipment, from steam heating and water supply to fire extinguishers. The wheel was a quick and simple control of a valve for any gas, liquid or chemical under pressure. As banks became more important and robberies increased, they adopted wheel-locking safes to protect valuables, sometimes of giant size. By such means, the leading industrialized nations had virtual control over environments both internal and external to the human body by the middle of the 20th century.

Control of hostile environments
The late 20th century gave new challenges to man. Sir Edmund Hillary and Sherpa Tensing Norgay reached the peak of Everest in 1953 using oxygen cylinders with valves controlled by wheels. In the 1940s, the Frenchman Jacques Cousteau invented the aqualung, a portable underwater breathing apparatus. Professor Auguste Piccard, from Switzerland, dived to new depths in his bathyscaphe and revealed some of the wonders of the deep ocean. Firefighters and those working with extremely dangerous materials such as radioactive substances, all used portable cylinders. The biggest challenge came with space. The Russians launched Yuri Gagarin into orbit in 1961. The "hatch" principle of submarines was used in the new spacecraft. The experiment succeeded and all manned journeys in space, including those to the moon from 1969, used the wheel for protection. Man had managed to survive, in the final challenge, the space that surrounds the Earth.

As humans ventured out from Earth to the space beyond, the wheel continued to play an important part in navigation, helping the space probe Voyager to explore further than humanity has ever ventured before.

When ancient peoples came to the point where they were able to control the time and place where they would eat, they had taken the first steps to controlling the environment that surrounded them. It was their choice to use or misuse it. This way of life remains to this day close to nature. Developed or developing cultures chose another course. The chance discovery of strains of grass which could be planted and tended led to the layout of fields over larger and larger areas. Over a period of 70 years, the average person requires about 220 tons (200 metric tons) of food, much of the energy from it going to heat their body. A population is directly linked to the amount of food available. The grinding-wheel and the wheelbarrow (believed to have come from China originally) were the first steps toward improving the quantity of food produced. As cultures developed in both the East and West, flat land was turned over to food, and the hills and forests to domesticated animals. Little changed for over 1,700 years.

The Agrarian Revolution

The basic tool for agriculture remained the wheeled plough, and mechanical help in grinding corn was provided by windmills. In about 1720, a lawyer in England called Jethro Tull invented a new type of wheeled plough and a wheeled seed drill. With its curved blades, the plough was able to tear strong turf and break the ground well below the surface. He found that by using the drill to sow regularly and deep, a better crop was produced. He used what was left over from the harvest as silage and bedding for the animals. Tull's strange behavior attracted the attention of two landowners who saw that planned sowing and full use of the crop improved both the value and quality of the harvest. Experiments showed that feeding certain crops to animals increased their size and yield. Wright introduced a more effective seed drill in 1787, using a handwheel to determine regular seed distribution. By the end of the 18th century, this revolution in food production spread across Europe and America.

The seed drill of the 18th century, invented by Jethro Tull, with large ironclad wooden wheels, was the first step on the road to modern scientific farming.

Mechanical transport and implements

Agriculture grew from a local to an international industry in the space of only 200 years. First with steam ploughs and then with traction engines, mechanization made it possible to harvest vast areas in ever shorter times. The use of ordinary, rimmed wheels was sometimes impossible because the land was so variable. The traction engine, driven by a steam engine, was fitted with a new innovation, caterpillar tracks which ran over the ground, allowing the wheel-base of the machine to be flexible according to the terrain. Using a side band over the flywheel, the engine could also be connected to a range of other agricultural machinery such as harvesters, lifts or bailers. The first gasoline-driven tractors appeared by 1900 and early combine harvesters were used within 20 years. The slim design of the tractor and rear balance of two huge wheels enabled it to maneuver with ease on both earth and roads in most weathers. With such machines, capable of working over miles of land in a single day, one farmer could now accomplish what it had taken dozens to do 50 years previously.

The traction engine, a common sight in the countryside 50 years ago, is now used only for display. Steam-powered, for years it was the only big labor-saving engine in modern farming. Note the huge flywheel above the rear wheel.

A combine harvester, capable of undertaking a number of jobs mechanically, is operated by a single person. Its widespread use changed the look of the countryside, giving rise to huge fields of one crop, as in this vast wheatfield in Oregon.

Results of new applications

The mechanization of farming had two major effects. It changed the look of the countryside forever. Small fields were joined up into larger plots for single crops (a monoculture) harvested by a small number of workers. The invention of the lawnmower in 1830 and the mechanical digger in the 1870s allowed vast areas to be cleared. These changes made it possible to produce crops at lower cost. But sustaining a high yield from the land had a price, once artificial fertilizers, delivered by wheeled vehicles, were introduced in 1946.

For most of the 19th century, transport of goods and the mechanical power to make them, were based on water – whether by barge or ship, or by the use of the steam-turbine or steam engine. Understanding of the properties of natural gas and oil led to the invention of the internal combustion engine in 1885 and the diesel engine in 1893. The use of wheels in a new range of vehicles, machines and processes brought huge social change within a century. The community vehicle gave way to one controlled by individuals.

First flight by Wilbur and Orville Wright, at Kitty Hawk, North Carolina, December 1903. Though their airplane stayed in the air for only a few minutes, the Wright brothers' flight became one of the key events of the 20th century by proving that, with mechanical means, the air could be conquered.

Another surge of transport by land, sea and air

Towards the end of the 19th century, road vehicles had continued to evolve. New machines included open and closed four-wheel carriages, and the two-wheeled hansom cab, all driven by horses. A new form of transport called the bicycle reached the height of popularity in the 1880s, when John Dunlop and Charles Goodyear introduced the air-filled rubber tire. The idea of a horseless self-controlled carriage powered by an engine led to the steam car. Though limited in their range by the water they had to carry, for the twenty years from 1880 to 1900 these cars were able to compete with the new motor car. All this changed in 1912 in America, when Henry Ford introduced the Model T, a cheap, efficient motor car. It sold in millions, especially after it was made weatherproof by adding windows and a roof. A whole range of standard vehicles followed – buses, trucks and vans. Electricity was used on steep gradients to power wheeled trolley buses, cable cars and streetcars in cities. The bicycle became the motorcycle and the Wright brothers pioneered the wheeled airplane in 1904.

The "Sunraycer," General Motors' solar-powered car, built in 1987, could be the future trend for wheeled vehicles and promises a revival of the flywheel.

Motor vehicles in war

As well as peaceful benefits, the new motor vehicles made a huge difference in the power of nations. During the First World War, which ended in 1918, tanks, trucks, cars, motorcycles and airplanes all took part in combat. The speed and destructive power of soldiers and machines and the weapons and armaments carried or pulled by them was awesome. At home, wheeled vehicles assisted in the supply of the materials needed for total war. The idea of the "Blitzkrieg" or completely mobile warfare was refined in the 1920s and 1930s. All soldiers and material necessary for war could be delivered at will to almost anywhere on Earth. The only possible counter to such power was nature itself, in terms of the weather. New inventions using wheels all sought to reduce the interference of the weather in combat. These included mobile radar, the self-righting compass and the telephone. In the Vietnam war, the United States even tried to change the climate itself, by using airplanes to seed the clouds with chemicals. In more recent conflicts, the wheeled vehicle remains the most effective means of waging war.

After the First World War, multi-wheeled vehicles, such as this German tank fitted with caterpillar tracks, were developed by armed forces all over the world, playing a crucial role in modern mobile warfare.

Modern wheels in peacetime

In everyday life, the use of the wheel was greatly extended in the 20th century. A number of uses are developments of old ideas, such as the rotary plough and the wristwatch. Entirely new worldwide industries have been established using wheels in just over 100 years. These include motion pictures, television (originally transmitted using a revolving disc and series of wheels), mobile furniture, the video and record industries. The wheel remains the key element in a whole range of products with mechanical parts. Medicine uses gurneys, wheelchairs, and pulleys for limb injuries, ambulances and lifts. Modern shopping and distribution use the trolley and forklift truck respectively. Fairgrounds use the ferris wheel and merry-go-round. On the tarmac of roads, signs are painted by wheeled markers and steamrollers smooth out hot bitumen. Vital oil and gas pipe-lines are regulated by wheeled valves. Reservoirs and dams still have their water controlled by wheels operated by hand. Without the wheel modern life would be little more advanced than ancient times.

Through to the end of the 19th century, there had been little change in building methods. Almost all buildings in towns and cities were largely built by hand. The machinery used, such as the crane and the pulley, though modern, was of ancient origin. By 1900, the major cities of the modern world were established, with the exception of Johannesburg, South Africa, which was to develop only as a result of the discovery and exploitation of local gold and diamond resources. The most populated urban areas remained where water transport was good and were built on rivers, lakes or seacoasts. It was only after 1920 that motor transport made a substantial impact on the planning and location of major cities.

The famous and impressive skyline of New York, on Manhatten Island, was the gateway to America for millions of emigrants from across the globe.

The city as port. The liner SS *Queen Mary* returns to New York with U.S. soldiers aboard, after World War II.

Moving the earth

Development and construction in cities began to change in 1884 when the Home Insurance Building in Chicago, considered the first skyscraper, was completed. It broke the 10-story barrier and was, in part, made possible by the invention of the elevator by Elisha Graves Otis in America in 1852. Originally driven by steam, electrically powered elevators became common early in this century. Steam shovels, which dug out foundations, remained fixed until 1895, when the rotary platform was invented in England. The basic machine, a crane or shovel, was now mounted on a three- or four-legged wheelbase, pinned to a revolving platform to allow a full turn. This mobility not only speeded up the process of unloading cargoes at busy city ports, but also made it possible to build quickly within the confines of modern city streets. It was this development, as much as the ingenuity of engineers, architects and the availability of new materials such as steel girders and reinforced concrete, which allowed the striking skyline of New York City to be built.

New developments

The last major wheel-based developments which transformed the possibilities of construction, the bulldozer and JCB, only came into use after 1945. Caterpillar tracks had appeared on steam machinery as early as 1911, but the demands for new roads required heavy, versatile and mobile machines. The bulldozer, initially used by the U.S. Army in southeast Asia in World War II, was soon adopted for civilian use. The JCB, a digger or earth-mover, invented by John Bamford in Britain, made possible the transport of vast quantities of materials over a wide range of terrain and by the 1990s was one of the most common construction vehicles throughout the world. The 1960s and 1970s construction of a jungle city like Brasilia, capital of Brazil, or the development of Anchorage, Alaska, demonstrated that even in the most unlikely environments, substantial building was possible. That such development combined to destroy the natural landscape and wildlife and cause immense damage to traditional ways of living was overlooked or ignored in pursuit of short-term demands and the illusion that such widescale construction would solve problems, not create them. These projects coincided with pre-fabrication, whereby entire blocks of apartments and mobile homes could be made in pieces and then rapidly assembled on site. New multi-wheeled transporters made this possible and resulted in over half of all the buildings in America being put together in this way from the 1960s. The mobile home, which first appeared in the United States in the 1920s, became immensely popular, allowing people to move all over the country as they wished.

The price of development. Pressure by population and industry results in the clearance of large areas of land for building, as here in the Brazilian rainforest. Only recently has such development begun to cause serious concern over the environment.

Brasilia - this great, remote capital of Brazil developed in the 1960s was made possible by using wheeled vehicles.

Up to the 1830s, the idea of mass transport for pleasure was new. Few workers had vacations on a regular basis and possibilities for travel as part of a way of life were limited to a few wealthy people. In Europe, the "Grand Tour" of seeing the sites of ancient Rome or Greece was the first regular tourist trip. The introduction of mass transport, such as the railways, was stimulated by mass emigration from Europe to America. The first regular transatlantic crossings, introduced for the transport of mail and manufactured goods, became more important for the transportation of people and their possessions.

Steam turbines

In 1838, two giant steamships, the *Great Western* and *Sirius*, arrived in New York Harbor on the same day. The event captured the public imagination and delighted the railway company which had backed the designer of the *Great Western*, Isambard Kingdom Brunel. These two great ships were able to ferry passengers across the Atlantic in 18 days. Huge paddle wheels, powered by steam engines, made good speeds possible and proved the inspiration for an engine which would be used to power the great liners of the future – the turbine.

The steam turbine was perfected by Sir Charles Parsons in 1887. Its first application was for the production of electricity. The great fan-like wheels were rotated by steam pressure, the power driving a dynamo. This application was, and remains, the basis for hydroelectric production. In 1894, the first Parsons engine was used in a ship, the *Turbinia*. In 1897 the *Turbinia* managed a world record speed of 34 knots, making frequent voyages across large areas of ocean much more practical. The age of long-distance, high-speed water travel had arrived.

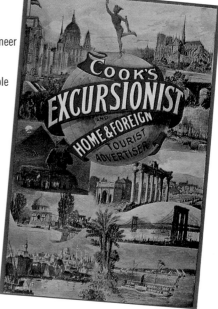

Thomas Cook, pioneer of mass travel, offered exotic locations to a whole range of tourists. Their high quality brochures and posters attracted many customers.

Early holiday trips

An English company, P & O, introduced the first cruise in the 1840s, to southern Russia. After the introduction of the factory acts in Britain, which limited working hours and proposed paid vacations, this form of vacation increased in popularity. It was, however, only in 1919 that regular daily passenger services were introduced – in Germany. By this time, large American, British, South American and German shipping companies had built luxury liners, such as the *Aquitania*, *Deutschland* and the ill-fated *Titanic*, to take hundreds of passengers to all parts of the globe in extreme comfort. Closer connections were formed between other forms of transport and ship and train connections became common by the 1930s.

The *Turbinia*, record-breaking turbine ship, under full speed. Using engines invented by Sir Charles Parsons, the ship caused a revolution in ship design.

Mass tourism

While aircraft were rapidly improved in the 1920s and 1930s, becoming enclosed and catering for limited numbers of passengers, they offered little competition to the hundreds of thousands of tourists being carried by wheeled transport and ship. Airports remained little more than collections of huts, though in the 1930s New York boasted a modern enclosed passenger terminal. The invention which changed air travel was the jet engine. The first such engine was tested by Heinkel, the German company, in 1939, and in 1941 the independently developed engine of Sir Frank Whittle was tested in Britain. At the end of World War II, both designs became widely available. Major aircraft companies – Boeing in the United States and Vickers in the United Kingdom – improved the originals and a whole series of aircraft with greater power and capacity went into service. Hundreds of thousands of new customers were attracted to fast air travel. The package tour was conceived and by 1961 over 30 million passengers were taken on vacation to all parts of the world. Up to the 1970s the great liners, such as the *France*, *QE II* and *Queen Mary* continued to compete with the airlines. In time, these great liners were phased out or limited to cruises for limited numbers of passengers. By the 1990s, air travel had become widely available and cheap.

The first two decades of the 20th century saw the introduction of the first great liners, such as RMS *Majestic (top)*, Cunard's *Mauritania(above)* and the German Lloyd lines *Kaiser Wilhelm*.

Aircraft such as the Boeing 747 Jumbo Jet, introduced in the 1970s, greatly increased the prospect of cheap air travel.

Problems in the air

Even with the introduction of new types of aircraft, such as the Jumbo wide-bodied jet or supersonic Concorde airliner, air travel remained very safe. In less than half a century, mass tourism became one of the world's largest industries. But during the 1970s and 1980s, air travel faced a new threat – the terrorist and hijacker. Tourist or business aircraft became the target of a number of terror campaigns. During the 1991 Gulf War, this concern reached crisis point as millions stayed away from air transport, fearing terror attacks. Yet air travel remains the most popular and still the safest method of transporting millions to vacation destinations, millions of tons of freight, and food to thousands affected by disasters.

anesthetic A means of producing loss of feeling or sensation in the body by the use of natural or synthetic drugs or gases. The idea of using drugs or gases was practiced in Asia and South America thousands of years ago.

capitalism A method of economic organization which depends on the production of goods by the use or investment of large sums of money, or capital. The majority of capitalist countries have a basis of private enterprise, rather than production paid for and run by the state.

chronometer A specially made time-piece which is both portable and accurate. It can compensate for heat and cold.

combine harvester A large wheeled vehicle which combines the different elements of various machines. It commonly includes a cutter (front rotary blades), a thresher, a bailer and a hopper, producing bales or a continuous flow of the cut and threshed crop.

combustion engine An engine which works by igniting a mix of air and fuel within an enclosed cylinder, causing an explosion which drives a piston. This eventually drives the wheels.

Conquistadors The Spanish name given to the adventurers such as Cortés and Pisarro, and to conquerors of the South American lands in the 16th and 17th centuries.

dynamo Also known as a generator, it is a machine which changes mechanical energy into electrical energy by rotating a series of wires wound around an iron core between the poles of a magnet.

flywheel A heavy wheel which reg-ulates or balances the speed of a machine.

fusee The conical wheel of a watch or clock which balances the power of the mainspring.

hair-spring The fine hair-like spring on the balance wheel of a watch.

jet engine Thrust, or movement, is created by the expulsion of gases from a turbine. Air is taken in at the front of the engine to a combustion chamber. Here fuel is ignited, causing greatly expanded (and therefore high speed) air to escape from a rear nozzle, moving the plane forward.

latitude The distance of an object on the Earth's surface from the equator, measured by imaginary lines on the surface about 69 miles (110 km) apart.

liner The name given to large steam-driven ocean-going passenger ships. Liners such as the *Mauritania* and the *Deutschland* were built before the First World War and were both large and luxurious.

longitude The distance along the Equator, measured in degrees, east or west of the Prime Meridian (in Greenwich, London).

Mesopotamia Present-day Iraq, it is the region between the Tigris and Euphrates rivers where the Assyrian, Babylonian and Sumerian civilizations developed from about 2000 B.C.

monoculture The use of land for a single crop or product. The earliest examples include vines (for wine) in France, Italy and Germany where large areas were devoted to the growing of grapes from the time of the ancient Romans. Since 1945 the term has been used for vast fields of wheat, barley and similar crops.

New Stone Age Known as the Neolithic, this era saw the first domestication of animals, the beginning of pottery, and the first permanent towns. It covers a period between 7000 and 1800 BC.

Old Stone Age Also known as the Paleolithic era. This period began over 600,000 years ago and marks the origins of human tool making, use of fire, and the earliest use of stone as a material. It covers all human history to about 10,000 B.C.

pendulum A rod or rods which are fitted with weights to swing freely below a clock mechanism. In the 18th century they were made of metals which, when combined, compensated for expansion and contraction with surrounding temperature.

Roman Empire The ancient Roman civilization was founded in Italy about 500 B.C. In about A.D. 350 it was divided into a Western and Eastern empire. One of the most stable periods in history, the empire extended across much of the known world until the fall of Rome in A.D. 476. The Eastern Empire lasted until the capture of Constantinople (Istanbul) by the Ottomans in 1453.

sluice An artificial floodgate for controlling water flow.

smelting The process of separating metal from its impurities. The metal and impurities have different weights when molten, and when heated the slag rises to the surface. It can then be skimmed off, leaving pure metal.

Sumerians The earliest civilization in Iran and Iraq, dating from as early as 5000 B.C. They were the earliest known users of the plough, chariot and potter's wheel. They built stepped temples known as ziggurats and they invented cuneiform writing.

terrorism The term applied to any act by an individual or group which frightens or terrorizes people, usually for political ends.

traction engine An early steam vehicle used on roads and farms to drive heavy machinery. Driven by a steam engine, it commonly had two giant rear wheels, and two smaller front wheels. The rear wheels were fixed, while those at the front used a steering wheel for direction.

turbine A motor which is driven or rotated by the force of water, steam or gas on the rotors of a wheel, much like the action of water on a waterwheel. After the source of power became gas (produced by burning oil fuel with air in a chamber) it was developed as the basis for the jet engine.

windlass A cylinder with a rope or chain, for raising weights, which is turned by a wheel or lever.

FURTHER READING

Davies, Eryl. TRANSPORT: On Land, Road and Rail (New York: Watts, Franklin, Inc., 1992).

Graham, Ian. TRANSPORTATION (Madison, NJ: Steck-Vaughn Company, 1993).

Spangenburg, Ray and Kit Moser. THE HISTORY OF SCIENCE IN THE NINETEENTH CENTURY (New York: Facts On File, 1993).

——————— . THE HISTORY OF SCIENCE FROM 1895–1945 (New York: Facts On File, 1994).

——————— . THE HISTORY OF SCIENCE FROM 1946 to the 1990s (New York: Facts On File, 1994).